ISRAEL

TIGER BOOKS INTERNATIONAL

Text
Fabio Bourbon

Graphic design
Patrizia Balocco

Contents

2-3 *The Old Town of Jerusalem is still situated within its medieval walls. Just right of center, you can see the golden dome of the Omar Mosque.*

4-5 *With long ringlets covering their ears, several young students of the Talmud Torah Shomrei Hachomot School eagerly pose for a photograph.*

6 *Several ritual objects such as the* Tefillin, *a small box containing fragments of the Torah, and the* Tallit, *the fringed prayer shawl, are worn by a rabbi during prayers.*

7 *An ancient minaret in the Old Town stands out against the majestic golden dome of the Omar Mosque, one of the symbols of Jerusalem.*

8-9 *A spectacular Roman aqueduct, the arches of which are still partially embedded in the sand, crosses the desert near Ceasarea.*

10-11 *A narrow strip of asphalt crosses the immense desolation of the Judean desert; for approximately three hundred days a year, the sun hammers down, scorching the air.*

12-13 *The view from from Mount Tabor includes this fertile stretch of land; Israeli agriculture has very much improved in recent years.*

14-15 *The Beatitudes Chapel was built in 1937 near Lake Tiberias, on the hill where, tradition tells us, Jesus held the Sermon on the Mount.*

The Editor wishes to give special thanks for their collaboration to: Raphael Gamzo of the Israeli Embassy in Italy, the cultural office; Shemi Tzur of the Foreign Affairs Ministry, Ofra Farhi, the Ottolenghi family, and Dario Colombo.

This edition published in 1993 by TIGER BOOKS INTERNATIONAL PLC, 26a York Street Twickenham TW1 3LJ, England.

First published by Edizioni White Star.
Title of the original edition
Israele, una terra antica per una giovane nazione.

Via Candido Sassone 24, 13100 Vercelli, Italy.

ISBN 1-85501-296-0

Printed in Singapore
Color separations by Magenta, Lit. Con., Singapore.

Introduction

To the far east, beyond the Mediterranean, past the sunburnt beaches of Africa, on the other side of mythic Greece and the historic islands of Cyprus and Rhodes, lies Israel — a land both antique and modern at the same time. It is antique because it is here where the sunrise of civilization began and where the Patriarchs laid the foundations of Jewish monotheism. It is here where King David built his realm, and Jesus carried out his mission. It is antique because it gave birth to civilizations and short-lived empires and then fell into complete oblivion. It is new because in this century, an entire nation has been restored, and there is a rebirth of hope and dignity for an entire people. It is new because with the hundreds of kibbutzim a new way of living has been founded. After centuries of abandonment, the land is covered again with fertile fields. Above all, it is a new land because the inhabitants are a newly immigrated cosmopolitan people from over seventy countries; they have been attracted to Israel by the promise of its Biblical prophecy.

The length of Israel is 248 miles. Its width varies from 8 to 68 miles, but the historical depth of this country is 5,000 years. From its desert sands to the ocean gulfs to the silent crevices of its grottos and caves, reminders of the past are everywhere. They range from Israelite fortresses and Roman amphitheaters to Byzantine churches, Nabatean cities, and castles from the Crusades.

However, only the human surroundings are able to give us an adequate idea of this small universe, where nature seems to offer to each person a climate and atmosphere suited to his needs.

Land of exile, Israël is also a land of contrasts, in which contradictory elements exist together — the past and the future, the West and the East, mystics and technocrats, believers and agnostics. Israel cultivates paradoxes; it is a recently formed state but it already possesses an avant-garde technology. Its people are passionately launched towards the future but have not forgotten for a single moment their earliest history, for that is what links them to their spiritual roots and resources.

This strip of land is a melting pot where one can

find a universal unity and a wealth of unprecedented social experience. This is a country that for years was on the front pages of newspapers all over the world almost every day, yet the land stretches only as far as the eye can see. There is the southern Mediterranean Sea, the green strips of fields along the coast, and the barren mountains of Judea and Samaria. Lebanon is to the north; Syria and Jordan lie to the east; and to the south lies the dazzling Negev desert, which borders the Egyptian Sinai. Upper Galilee in the north is marked by deep depressions and low spurs which are so intensely cultivated that this region is regarded as the land of olive and fruit trees. The uneven landscape of Samaria resembles that of Upper Galilee, while the mountains of Judaea are inaccessible. The Golan Heights, which rise nearby, can be distinguished by old, inactive volcanos, reminders of complex geological eras. The coastal lowlands stretch from the foot of Mount Carmel to the Gaza Strip. The land is extremely fertile, with cypress, eucalyptus, sycamore, date, and palm trees, and orange groves that yield fruit even in the middle of winter. The highest point in the region is the 3,930-feet-high Mount Meron in Galilee, while Sedom, at 1,284 feet below sea level, represents the lowest point. Israel encompasses only 7,878 square miles and it is probably the only country in the world to have no precisely defined boundaries, as a consequence of the Six-Day War and the still unresolved question of the disputed territories. Four millions Jews and more than 700,000 Arabs live in this tiny land of contention. In addition, another 1.3 million people have been living in the territories of Jordan, the Gaza Strip, and the Golan Heights disputed since 1967.

There are different cultural groups in this small country, where memories of Christianity influence the interpretation of new symbols, and politics struggle with the old. But herein lies the true secret of Israel. For its extraordinary compactness, the country is extremely rich in both distinguishing features and contradictions and also in its different peoples and customs. All of these elements are contained within a miniature existence. In this land of Zion, variety does not necessarily mean vastness, but instead, it represents an endless range of nuances. Ever since the Jews who had been dispersed around the world assembled in this country where their history began, extremely different cultural groups have been springing up in Israel, creating a culturally diverse society. This land of immigrants is like a historic jigsaw puzzle that human will has been trying to reassemble with great effort. In Israel, Jews are no longer simply Jews but different types of Jews. They are loved, hated, and feared because of their role in leading the country and its military

16 *North of the Dead Sea, along the road from Jerusalem, is the ancient city of Jericho, which, according to Biblical tradition, was conquered by Joshua around the 13th century B.C. During the Roman era, Herod the Great enriched the city with magnificent buildings, after which it became an important Episcopal residence during the Christian era. However, a slow but unavoidable decline began after the Crusades, transforming it gradually into an Arab city. Since 1967, it has belonged to Israel, as a result of the victorious Six-Day War. Archeological excavations have uncovered a 6th-century synagogue and the ruins of the palace of Isham, an Arab caliph of the 8th century. In addition to numerous architectural elements, the famous Tree of Life mosaic is splendidly preserved, a symbol frequently adopted in the Mediterranean area.*

power. From the inside, Israel is a fractional world whose history, political life, and ethnic composition are marked by profound divisions. Israelis of Arab or European origin, Kurds and Iraqis, Americans and Russians, Moroccans and Yemenites tenaciously protect the legacy of their respective cultural traditions, which have been able to coexist only as a result of complex internal diplomatic relations. Despite countless differences, they all try to imagine a common future and to create a new life. Their differences of language, custom, and folklore bring about a coexistence fortified by potentiality that enriches the cultural life of the country.

Even from a strictly historical point of view, this corner of the Middle East is like a huge mosaic of contrasting events dating back to the dawn of civilization. More than 4,000 years ago, a man set off with his flock from Ur, in Chaldea, to settle in Be'er Sheva. His name was Abraham; he was the first Patriarch of Judaism. Nineteen centuries later, Mary, the wife of Joseph, a carpenter from Nazareth in Galilee, bore a son — Jesus. In the year 622, a young man crossed the desert, his heart overflowing with visions and conviction, to preach his faith in Allah, the one and only God. He was Mohammed, the Prophet of Islam. As you can see, over the centuries, Israel has been a land of conflict but at the same time of crucial meetings. The Bible describes it as a land of milk and honey, but until recent times, it was nothing but a desert of marshes and barren lands. Only its strategic location can explain why the Promised Land of the Jews has been object of contention and imperial ambition throughout its history. There have been Egyptians, Assyrians, Babylonians, Persians, Greeks, and Romans, followed by Byzantines, Arabs, Crusaders, Mamelukes, and Ottomans. Even the English considered the conquest of Israel to be indispensable for consolidating their empire.

Trying to summarize the remote history of the Jewish people is like writing the Old Testament in the form of a school textbook. On the other hand, the Bible should actually be your guide if you want to get to know Israel, because its history is more likely to inspire the mystic than the sociologist. Biblical reminiscences are everywhere. They are in the places where King David lived, where the prophet Isaiah used to pray, and where the Maccabees rebelled. This harsh land, which has been the land of patriarchs, kings, prophets, and of the Messiah, does not fall into any rational and logical categories. The Pentateuch describes in detail how the family of Jacob, who was Isaac's son and Abraham's grandson, settled in Egypt. After struggling with an angel, Jacob was called Israel,

17 *Isham's Palace, built in the Byzantine style with Islamic influence, was partially destroyed by an earthquake in 747 B.C. Archeological excavations revealed part of the ruins of the palace; these are among the most interesting finds in Israel.*

which means "God has won." The Pharaoh did not view the spreading of the Hebrews throughout Egypt with favor, nor did he tolerate their growing influence in society, their different customs, and their refusal to abide by his laws. He began to hinder them by trying to reduce their birthrate and forcing them to do humiliating jobs. This persecution went on for four centuries, until Moses decided to free his people from slavery and lead them to the land of Canaan, the "Promised Land." In the desert, God showed himself to Moses and gave him the Tablets of the Law, the Torah, which was to turn Israel into "a people who cannot be conceived amidst other nations." Once they reached Canaan and had conquered Jericho, the Hebrews settled in the western Jordan basin. According to tradition, they consolidated their conquests between 1200 and 1100 B.C. At the time of the judges and under Kings Saul, David, and Solomon, they divided into twelve tribes and turned to a completely sedentary life. A political-religious organization was created around Jerusalem and the First Temple. Even after the Babylonian invasion and the deportation to Mesopotamia, the desire to go back to Zion, fostered by the Prophets, remained alive. When Babylonia was conquered by Cyrus and the Hebrews were freed from exile, they managed to re-establish their community in Judea, although it was much smaller than the previous one. In 65 B.C., Pompey started the Roman penetration of the land, which led to the creation of the Kingdom of Herod the Great, favoured by the leader of the Romans. Meanwhile, a serious ethical and cultural crisis was growing in Palestine as a result of the divisions of the various ethnic groups and the spreading of Christianity. Initially divided into three parts and then reunified, the Hebrews of Palestine became more and more impatient with the Caesars' domination and organized an uprising that was bloodily repelled by Titus in 70 A.D., destroying Jerusalem and the Temple. After a futile resistance that went on for about sixty years, the surviving Jews began the Diaspora.

Over the following eighteen centuries, the history of Israel tells us of a restless land where Jews, Christians, and Muslims professed their beliefs and traveled on pilgrimages. It is a land first dominated by the Roman, then Islamic caliph, then crusaders and Moslem again, Napoleonic troops, then followed by Ottoman pashas, and finally, British imperialists. Yet the country was never a nation until one century ago, when the first Jewish pioneers, driven out of Russia and Poland by the pogroms, on one hand and from Yemen on the other hand, began to settle in the Promised Land.

Since the destruction of the second Temple, the hope of returning to Zion has been the primary moving

18 left *The Bar'am Synagogue is the most well preserved and the most ancient in Israel; its ruins date back to the beginning of the third century B.C.*

18 right *The Beth She'arim necropolis is one of the most extraordinary archeological sites in Israel; many of the grand sarcophogi in the underground halls are decorated with strange bas-reliefs of lions, bulls, and eagles.*

19 top *After the pillage of Jerusalem in 70 A.D., Beth She'arim became the headquarters of the Sanhedrin and the main cultural center of Palestine. More than twenty monumental gates lead to the enormous underground cemetery excavated following this event.*

19 middle *The magnificent floor of the Beth Aleph Synagogue, from the 6th century A.D., is the most well preserved of its kind. It was discovered in 1928, but a long period of restoration was necessary before it could be shown to the public.*

19 bottom *Deep in the hills, the archeological excavations of the Beth She'arim catacombs have opened up many miles of tunnels filled with hundreds of sarcophagi.*

20-21 *Acre, one of the most ancient cities in the world, is situated along the Bay of Haifa and today is the main fishing center of the country. It was the ancient city of Saint-Jean-d'Acre during the Crusades; the famous underground churches and the walls are still well preserved.*

spirit of Judaism. The Jews always used to pray looking eastward, nursing their homesickness countless times by saying, "Next year in Jerusalem!" This is a unique phenomenon in the history of a people. This faith in homecoming kept the Jewish people pure and united despite all of the persecutions they suffered. Zionism is therefore not a new concept in the history of Judaism. Instead, it is the modern manifestation of a very ancient feeling. Until the eve of World War II, the pioneers settled in the desert and marshy lands with the goal of creating an ethically perfect and just society, a Utopia for an utterly new people. By the late 1930s, the number of Jews that had come to Palestine reached half a million. Meanwhile, anti-Semitism, which has plagued the people of David throughout history, was progressively spreading all over Europe. With Nazism began the most tragic and dramatic period in the history of the Jewish people. Six million Jews died in the concentration camps. Those who survived the Holocaust did not give up hope, and on May 14, 1948, the foundation of the State of Israel was proclaimed by virtue "of the natural and historical right of the Jewish people and of the resolution of the United Nations." On the date of the proclamation of independence, the neighboring Arab states moved to attack. This war, which is called the "War of Independence," was the first, but also the hardest, of a series of armed conflicts involving Israel and the Arab world. The following years were devoted to the two tasks of consolidating the country's position on international levels and dealing with internal problems. Special emphasis was placed on economic and social issues, aimed at preparing the young nation for the growing flood of immigrants. From the very first day of Israel's independent existence, the Arab world shunned the idea of a Jewish nation in the Middle East as if it were a thorn in its side.

In 1956, 1967, and 1973, Israel and its hostile neighboring countries addressed the question on the battlefield. Egypt lost the Suez War in 1956, but, as a consequence of strong international pressures, the government of Ben Gurion gave the Sinai back to the country. Eleven years later, the so-called "Six-Day War" broke out, during which the Israeli army, " Tsahal ", demonstrated its efficiency by defeating not only the Egyptian armies in the south, the Syrian armies in the north but also the Jordanian army in the east. It was during this lightning-fast military campaign that Israel took possession of the old part of Jerusalem, which encloses the sacred monuments of Judaism. Until then, like Berlin, Jerusalem had been divided into two parts. A few days after the end of the war, the Star of David waved over the reunified city, while soldiers and civilians radiant with joy embraced one another in front of the Wailing

Wall. With the glorious excitement over this short-lived victory came the illusion of Israel's invincibility. On October 6, 1973, Yom Kippur, (the most solemn day of the Jewish year, for which all activity is interrupted), the Egyptian and Syrian armies took the offensive. The quick, bold reaction of Israel enabled "Tsahal" to take the initiative again and finally to prevail. The Yom Kippur War cost Israel 3,000 lives and brought to light the idea of the country's precariousness and the possibility of annihilation. Nevertheless, the country proved that it was able to react swiftly and effectively.

In more recent years, Prime Minister Menachem Begin signed the Camp David agreement, and Egypt and Israel have even established friendly diplomatic relations. Many problems remain unsolved, but the dream of a global solution no longer seems unthinkable since Arabs, Palestinians, and Israelis decided to do what was once thought to be impossible — sit together at the negotiating table. Maybe the time has come to find an answer to the question of an anguished Ben Gurion: "With whom will we hold a dialogue if we do not attempt to find a reliable interlocutor?"

Only if you know in detail the tormented history of this young nation can you fully understand the proportions of Israel's economic boom. What has characterized the country's economy has been the acceleration of development over the last decades. Although the growth has been periodically interrupted by serious crises, industrial production is now thirteen times as great as thirty years ago. However, during the first years of independence, there was great austerity, and only after a while was there any regularity in the budget.

This stability was fostered, in large part, by the considerable contribution of the kibbutzim, strongholds of human and material resources and among the most interesting and original realities of modern Zionism. Kibbutz is a Hebrew term meaning "group" and stems from a collectivistic agricultural-industrial system upon which the reclamation of Israel's land has been partially based. It is hard to say whether it was the urgency of the situation or the development of a new social awareness that made the greater contribution to this phenomenon. Certainly, this trend took shape at the beginning of the century with the development of Zionism. In 1901, the National Fund was created for land purchases in Palestine to be rented to tenants. The idea of establishing working "communes" became a reality in 1909, when the first actual kibbutz, Degania, settled on its own estate to launch a rather precarious farm. Today, Degania is one of the most thriving villages in Israel. After this success, the new communities began to spread. By 1918, about thirty kibbutzim had been created, and thirty years later, on

the eve of independence, more than a hundred communities had developed, scattered through various parts of Israel. They were prosperous "islands," successful pilot-experiments in the field of industrial and agricultural economy. But one must be reminded that in a climate of war, they had to function above all as fortified outposts able to resist possible attacks. This characteristic remained one of their distinguishing features until the Six-Day War.

Initially created for agriculture, numerous kibbutzim also developed various industrial or handicraft activities which decidedly contributed to their prosperity. The fact that today many of the kibbutzim are secure economically derives also from their ability to make changes even when this involves painful loss. Work on a wage basis had to be reintroduced, and the employment of Arab manpower became necessary. Today, although life in the kibbutz is still inspired by the old collectivistic ethics, the existence of the *haver* (inhabitant) is enlivened by clubs, swimming pools, libraries, and museums and has little in common with the founders' Spartan beginnings. Cultural activities occupy a very important place in the modern kibbutz. Conferences, concerts, exhibitions, excursions, archeological and environmental studies are pleasant ways to spend one's free time.

Things have also changed at the national level. In Israel, after the heroic age of ideologists and pioneers, there is now emerging an era of technocrats and large-scale planning. Yet the economic importance of the kibbutz is far from being negligible for a population that amounts to no more than three percent of the whole. Intensive methods in agriculture and highly advanced technologies in industry make these communities actual laboratories of progressive economy.

The greatest success of the kibbutz, however, is the upbringing of the children known as "children of the dream." Born in a land which is finally their own, the young people feel at ease in a landscape made up of sun, sea, and rolling hills. The mixture of ethnic groups has given them a vigor their parents never had. Their spare and brusque way of speaking ignores the soft inflections of languages spoken by the Jews in exile, the polite subtleties of Jewish gestures, and the exhausting acrobatics of a dialect. As modern children of Zion, they have been the first to learn the language of their Biblical forefathers from birth. It was not by chance that, after arriving in this land from the four corners of the earth with the aim of creating a new homeland, the first thing the Jews of Israel wanted to do was bring their ancient language back to life. The language, spoken twenty-five centuries before the prophets, had survived only in prayers and lamentations, in the liturgies of the synagogue, or as a subject of scholarly study. The major problem for modern Israel's founders was to make the archaic language current and usable so that it could then be taught to a people that had forgotten even its most basic rules. Despite such evident difficulties, the objective was brilliantly achieved, and today, Hebrew is the national language taught at school, spoken in cafés and at the stadium, used for scientific research, etc. This was not easy — especially for the older people. A well-known joke says that Israel is the only place in the world where children sometimes teach their parents how to talk.

In this young nation, where the spoken language is thousands of years old, in this chaos of different accents and distinguishing physical features, in this land were most of the history of the Jewish people took place, the youth are passionately trying to dig out the archives of their history, saving every trace of their past from the desert sand. Here, more than anywhere else, archeology possesses the absolute value of recovering one's origins and national identity. That is why only here is the study of ancient finds at the same time a need and a pastime, a science and a national sport. From the walls of Tiberias to the ruins of Avdat, from the necropolis of Sanhedria to the amphitheater of Caesarea, the Israelis feel the need to understand the intricacies of their past as a part of their search for unity. Archeology represents an essential way of recovering tradition, an important investigation into Jewish heritage, and an attempt to justify their rights to the country, so frequently claimed in the various historical phases. Consequently, it is not by chance that, starting with the declaration of independence in 1948, all national symbols have been inspired by archeological discoveries. From the State seal (the Menorah) to the minting dye for coins, these symbols have become famous among numismatists all over the world for the beauty of their design.

The national identity and a common historical legacy represent, therefore, a fundamental problem for the existence of a nation that sees its raison d'etre as the formation of a democratic and pluralistic society. Israel does not have to become endangered by intolerance or incomprehension of its own cultural roots. It must be strong both with the external world and at home. Since the Diaspora myth fostering Jewish unity against a basically hostile world no longer exists, the differentiated heritage of 2,000 years of assimilation and dispersion is acquiring more importance than ever.

You can easily distinguish between the Sephardim, the Jews from Arab countries, and the Ashkenazim, natives of central and eastern Europe.

23 top *From Jerusalem to Tiberias and from Judea to Negev, majestic monumental remains can be seen, evidence of the Roman domination under Pompey from 65 B.C., interrupted seven centuries later by the Islamic conquest.*

23 bottom *On the outskirts of Bet Shean, a small town situated in the Jordan valley and the Jezreel valley, various excavations have revealed stratifications belonging to different eras. The most impressive ruins are from the Roman era and comprise a theater and amphitheater as well as several well-preserved columns.*

22 *An ancient Philistine center, Ashqelon is a famous seaside resort in the southern part of the country.*

24-25 *For the Jewish people, religion permeates all aspects of life, be they individual or social. In this photograph, a family is assembled for the Seder, the commemorative feast celebrated during Passover.*

The Jews from Iraq are different from those who come from Yemen or Morocco, just as the Russians differ from the Rumanians or the Poles. Each group maintains and tries to hand down to the new generation the old ways of dressing, cooking, celebrating festivals, ways of living and dying. We could almost say that Israel is still a mythical country with a unique abstract entity that bears many names. The Jewish land is *eretz Israel*, the land that was promised by God to Jacob and to his descendants. The Roman name adopted by the Turks, Arabs, and English is Palestine, whereas the Christians call it the Holy Land. Similarly, you could choose from among any number of widespread stereotypical figures. Israel is either the heroic and besieged David or the armed and militaristic Goliath. It is the Holy Land of the Crusaders or the land of the pioneers who turned the desert into a garden. It is the battlefield of the Palestinian revolt or the Jewish State that has come back to life after eighteen centuries of foreign domination.

Apart from this, Israel is above all an astonishing human enigma, a tiny piece of land where over a hundred different ethnic groups live together. Jews and Muslims, Syrians, Lebanese, *masri* (Egyptians), and *ja'bari* (Iraqis) all immigrated between 1922 and 1948. There are desert Bedouins and there are Christians from all over the world, ranging from Ethiopian Copts, Maronites, and Armenians to American Mormons. And we cannot forget the minorities that have stood their ground regardless of the fact that they have been persecuted in their countries of origin. This list includes the Kurds, Druse, Circassians, Karaites, Samaritans, and even the Vietnamese "boat people."

The Jewish majority of the population, however, has the greatest number of different ethnic groups, although in principle the Jews can be basically divided into Ashkenazim and Sephardim. Actually, the difference between the European Jews, heirs of the Zionist pioneers, and those coming from the Muslim orient is not only religious and cultural but also political. For over thirty years, the Sephardim represented a "minor Israel" within a modern, technologically-advanced and highly westernized society. Their individualistic craftspeople were not suited to the collectivistic lifestyle of the kibbutz. The Yom Kippur War, which was won at tremendous risk and with terrible losses, marked the beginning of the Sephardic sector's political recovery in Jewish society. Today, being a Sephardic Jew has almost become fashionable. The most elegant shops in Tel Aviv as well as many successful small businesses and the best restaurants are run by Sephardim. The members of this group belong to the ruling class and promote their folklore with increasing success. Although there are still two rabbinates and two different cults, the gap between the two communities is being bridged thanks to mixed marriages and to a substantial equality of economic conditions.

But what still strikes the observer is the huge ethnic diversity among the Jews. In the streets of Tel Aviv, you can see the characteristic Chassidim of Eastern Europe, with long earlocks and mournful black clothes, or the dark Yemenites, who arrived in 1949 through a gigantic airlift operation called "Flying Carpet." You can see American blacks or amber-skinned Indians. The Iraqis, Iranians, Moroccans, and Kurds work together for Israel's future. The Ethiopian blacks who immigrated in 1984 thanks to another airlift — the "Operation Moses" — and in 1991 "Operation Solomon" create a colorful contrast with the Europeans, who often have fair hair and eyes. Masses of new immigrants come since 1980 from the ex Soviet Union: from Russia, Ukraine, the Baltic States as well as from Khazakistan and the Asian Republics. These groups have reached the land in waves at different times in history. The children and grandchildren of this multiracial patchwork are *sabra*, which means cactuses, since they were born in the desert and have been citizens of Israel from birth. They account for sixty per cent of the Jewish population and reflect its large ethnic variety by sharing a turbulent past and the awareness of belonging now to one nation. From this hopeful perspective, the words of Erez Bitton, a university professor, poet, and songwriter, sound like something more than a simple prophecy: "Our children will grow up differently. They will be neither Sephardim nor Ashkenazim. Only Israelis." For Bitton, as for thousands of Jews, this is a certainty clearer than dawn.

While a better future perhaps lies ahead, it is still evident that entire cities were created and developed on the basis of the various Jewish immigrations. Israel has become a concentration of various ethnic groups. Even among Palestinian Arabs, diversity predominates over homogeneity. Muslim and Christian communities live integrated together from the heights of Galilee to the Negev desert, dominion of the Bedouins. Moreover, there are Druse tribes which are divided into those who are faithful to Israel — e.g., those who live in Eastern Galilee and do their military service under the flag of the Star of David — and the Pro-Syrians, who live in the Golan villages.

Another difficult problem lies in the distinction between the so-called "Arabs of 1948," who remained in Israel when the state was being created, and the "Arabs of 1967," who have been living in a condition of military rule for over twenty years and fan the flames

of political tension in the Middle East. The former are citizens of Israel in every respect. They pay taxes, have an Israeli passport and the right to vote. But they do not do military service. The latter wait for a solution of "self rule" and meanwhile they have no political rights. Here lies a potential time bomb of unsolved tension which threatens to explode.

The variety of Israel exists also in the contrast between its cities. Tel Aviv, the Zionist city par excellence, was founded in 1909 — a time when the first Russian and Polish immigrants were arriving, with the idea of preparing a homeland for all their persecuted brothers. It is therefore a completely new metropolis, made up essentially of buildings that were rapidly erected to absorb the enormous waves of immigrants. However, the center of Tel Aviv retains some of the features of the first Russian settlement. There are two- or three-story houses with small arches, pediments, projecting balconies, and rounded roofs, which closely resemble houses from the last century in Odessa and other southern Ukrainian towns.

Tel Aviv, the real moving force of Israel's economic life, is a town with two faces. The first and most conspicuous is its pulsating and dynamic city center, with large streets teeming with cars, shops, movie houses, cafés, theaters, restaurants, large hotels, night clubs, museums, and cultural buildings. The heart of Tel Aviv beats at a nervous and frenetic rhythm typical of large metropolises. Yet greater Tel Aviv with the largest number of inhabitants in Israel has a chaotic and disordered structure. Looking at the city, which is so near the sea, you would guess it had been designed, built, and inhabited by people who were not very familiar with the sea. The eight-mile-long beach represents the second face of Tel Aviv. Slightly south of the metropolis is the harbor town of Jaffa, which has ancient Arab origins but is now inseparably connected to the modern urban center. It still maintains its exterior appearance, although it has become a bustling art, shopping, and entertainment location. Even an artistic quarter has developed here, with galleries and workshops exhibiting pottery, sculpture, painting, and carpets. If during the day, life flows quickly from one traffic jam to the other, the night reveals the authentic soul of the young metropolis. The streets in the city center light up as if it were daytime, and Tel Aviv becomes the New York City of Israel. The scandalized Rabbis of Jerusalem thunder with discontent, demanding the closing of all public places of amusement for the Jewish sabbath.

Jerusalem is only thirty-nine miles from Tel Aviv, yet the two cities are completely different worlds. They are connected by a modern motorway, which crosses the green plain covered with thriving kibbutzim, but they are separated by thousands of years of history. There is no chaotic disorder, no endless rows of ultramodern buildings overlooking the plain, but a succession of white houses on the various hills divided by deep, green valleys. Jerusalem combines all the contradictions of the country and of a good part of the Middle East in the most conspicuous way. It is the capital of the State and the holy city for three religions and therefore a place of contention par excellence. It contains within itself all the various components and passions of Israel's society. The 15th-century earthworks include the Wailing Wall, the Holy Sepulchre, and the Omar Mosque. The most significant liturgies of the three monotheistic faiths are performed here. The complexity of the situation is revealed by the acts of devotion rather than by the monuments, notwithstanding their solemn holiness. On Fridays, the shops owned by the Muslims who live in the Old Town are closed, and 350,000 inhabitants — nearly a third of Jerusalem's population — celebrate the weekly festivity. From the minarets, muezzins invite people to pray, while the believers assemble in the large square in front of the Omar Mosque, where in the living rock are the footprints of Mohammed.

The following day is Saturday, the Jewish Sabbath, but already on Friday, early in the afternoon, the new city becomes empty and some old quarters such as the ultra-orthodox Mea Sharim, are surrounded by barriers. On Saturday morning, groups of believers walk quickly through the city's sleeping streets to reach the Wailing Wall, the last remains of the temple destroyed by Titus, and the symbolic center of Judaism. Here the Jews pray, rhythmically swaying forward and backward. Most of them are dressed according to the strictest rules of the Ashkenazic tradition, in long black overcoats and the characteristic hat. All day long, Jerusalem remains empty in an evident and sought-after contrast with the hedonistic and noisy sabbath of Tel Aviv. On Sunday morning, one can hear the bell tolling from the Old Town in Jerusalem, rocking this corner of the Middle East like a crib. A crowd of believers enters the Church of the Holy Sepulchre, and soon many groups form, following their own priests — the Catholic and the Orthodox, the Copt and the Protestant, in a puzzling variety of vestments and headgear. The same happens in all places that are sacred to Christianity and have witnessed the life and death of Jesus, whether it be Tiberias, Nazareth, or Bethlehem. If Tel Aviv is a lay city, lively and self-confident, dynamically oriented towards the uncertainties of the future, Jerusalem is the city of eternal certainties, religious ardor, and memory. As complementary realities, Tel Aviv and Jerusalem

26 *In a little more than forty years, Israel has fought six wars, and even though at present the country is involved in peace negotiations, it has never ceased to strengthen itself militarily, in the eventuality of another war. In a country obsessed by defense, it is no wonder that women are also actively involved in the military.*

embody the two forces that led to the creation of the modern State of Israel — Zionist ideology and religious tradition. Today, however, neither of these cities is able to determine on its own the future of a democratic and pluralistic society which can accept different ethnic groups while respecting their own identity. Today, Israel belongs to the ordinary people who live and work there and long for security and well being. Despite the existing gap, Tel Aviv and Jerusalem are symbols of the nation's human and social realities.

The Dead Sea combines, more than any other geographical place, the extreme yet fascinating physical reality of Israel. An anomaly, the lake is forty-seven miles long and eleven miles wide. Sunk between Israel and Jordan, the Dead Sea possesses the enchantment of a lunar landscape and of a glorious history. It witnessed the tragedies and victories of the Jewish people from the time of Abraham to the days of the kibbutz. It is a famous area for naturalistic and archeological excursions and a destination young tourists always include in their schedules. Moreover, this incredible stretch of water is an ore field that has no equal in nature. The particular weather conditions of the region have made it a unique health resort in the desert. It is famous for its mineral springs and spas with extraordinary effects.The name couldn't be more suitable; there is a total absence of life, which goes hand in hand with the fact that it is the lowest point on the earth's surface, 1,305 feet below sea level. The Dead Sea has twenty-five per cent salinity and an extraordinary degree of evaporation, ranging from two to twenty-five millimeters per day. That is why there is no vegetation and there are no fish. Swimming is forbidden along much of the coast. Swimming off shore is dangerous even though the water density pushes the body towards the surface and prevents sinking. Water swallowed accidentally could cause health problems. It is possible to bask in the sun without risking sunburn because the particular characteristics of the atmosphere filter the shortest ultraviolet rays. The air is heavy and seems to compress the horizon under a canopy of silence. Yet, what the figures cannot explain is that here, desolation reaches the boundaries of absolute poetry. Seen from far away, the Dead Sea is smooth, bright, and still, surrounded by sun-bleached, chalk-white crags, connotations of its rough, tridimensional reality portraying an imaginary landscape, a boundless surrealistic scenery. As soon as you drive into the large depression, you realize that in few other places in the world does geography become so explicitly real as here. It overcomes the physical boundaries of mountains, plains, rivers, and frontiers. From Nabi Maussa, where, according to tradition,

27 The green Tsahal uniform of the army is a daily feature of Israeli life; each citizen is a soldier on leave who can be called up at any moment. This continuous alternation between civil and military life renders the Tsahal a popular army — a democratic institution where all social differences are cancelled.

Moses's grave is situated in the ancient Baibars Mosque, you can see Jordan, Palestine, and the land of Israel as well as the square croplands of the Jordan Valley.

The flow of the river, surrounded by intense green scrub, stops a few feet from the Dead Sea and sinks into the dazzling yellow sand, leaving no trace of humidity. Its milky horizon vanishes towards the Negev, the large desert sprawling over the southern part of the country. It is an area where there is only one town — Be'er Sheva — which is still inhabited by many nomadic tribes of Arab Bedouins. Not far from the mouth of the Jordan are the Qumran caves, where the famous Dead Sea Scrolls were found and where the Essenes used to live. They were an austere religious sect whose members met to study the divine law together. Although during each excavating season, archeologists continue to find traces of Biblical events, with historical confirmation on one hand and divine mysteries on the other, this is not a paradise, nor has it ever been. Perhaps the Arab-Israeli problem is all here, in this tiny place that can be seen at a glance. It is not simply an economic or ideological question, and, at least to a certain extent, not simply a religious one. It is, instead, the possession of a land which is so desperately small. The Dead Sea is one of those places in the complex triangle of land called Israel where you can still hear the challenge of different languages.

At En Gedi, halfway up the long coastal road, there is a kibbutz. Even today, choosing to live there requires some of the visionary and absolutist courage that was once attributed to the prophets. Created in 1956 out of a military outpost which protected the border with Jordan, it is now inhabited by 200 full-time members and another 400 persons, including guests, visitors, and tourists. The kibbutz is green, spacious, and efficient, complete with swimming pools, gyms, and even a theater. The surrounding oasis has been declared a nature reserve. A unique combination of plants grows there, ranging from aquatic to desert vegetation and even some tropical species. Moreover, foxes, hyraxes, wolves, and leopards, as well as a large number of steinboks and birds, live in this lush garden. A meeting point of two different climates and landscapes — the Asiatic and the African — En Gedi owes its fortune to the presence of numerous springs and falls. The Song of Songs praised the delights of this oasis in the middle of the desert, which offered travelers a rest in cool and idyllic serenity. A determined human will has succeeded in creating something which closely resembles what we might imagine to be the Garden of Eden. Yet just a few feet from the greenhouses and flower beds, the borders of the kibbutz open onto

28 top *The Jordan valley enjoys a particularly flourishing agriculture, thanks to the combination of climate, geological features, humidity, and meteorological stability.*

28 bottom *A liquid disinfectant is sprayed on a banana plantation in the Degania kibbutz near Tiberias. Also grown in this area are dates, figs, pineapples, mangos, and papayas.*

29 top *The diamond industry, introduced into the modern Jewish state by Belgian and Dutch immigrants, has so greatly expanded that, in 1974, Israel became the world's main exporter of diamonds.*

29 bottom *Israel does not abound in raw materials, but has been able to overcome this fact by advanced technology in the industrial and scientific fields. Shown here is a solar power system at the Weizmann Institute of Rehovot.*

30-31 *The enormous tourist-commercial center of Kikar Atarim is one of the recent architectural developments that characterizes Tel Aviv today.*

nothingness. Not a single drop of rain falls for 360 days of the year. Some large thermal baths, wells, and pipes collect water from sulfurous springs. The long canal dug in the bed of the Dead Sea makes the water flow southward, thus preventing the basin from disappearing, leaving a huge stretch of rock and salt.

Even En Gedi, despite all its facilities, is marked by the fatigue of living in the desert, although every inhabitant of the bustling kibbutz would be ready to explain without hesitation why he or she has made such an extreme choice. In the first place, it is a civic duty, since the state needed a stable settlement at one of the most dangerous points along its borders, and second, because the oasis appears to each of them as one of the most beautiful places in the world, with the sweet and mysterious nature of mountains behind and the sea in front. The fact that not one single blade of grass can grow in the hard rock does not matter to them. Equally unimportant is that the sea is such a dense concentration of salts that it can not be considered water. The Dead Sea is immersed in the silence of past times sought by people discovering the depth of the soul.

Indeed, the Dead Sea has always been a theater of extreme feelings and actions. Its dramatic reputation dates back to Biblical times. Genesis tells us that Sodom, a small town on the southern coast, was swept away by divine wrath after various unsuccessful attempts at redemption. Still today, the harsh landscape surrounding its remains seems to bear the signs of the sulfuric rain and fire that marked the mountain. The first dynastic conflict that devastated Israel took place here. And it was here, in the oasis of En Gedi, that David found refuge from the anger of King Saul, and here that his life was spared. This was probably the only bloodless event that occurred in the desert of Judea. Its hard contours seem to have been designed for extreme situations and desperate choices.

Around A.D. 70, nearly 1,000 Jews rebelled against the Roman domination and shut themselves up in the impregnable Masada stronghold, which was built on a rock that juts out over the desert, facing the Dead Sea. The lone rock stands out as a proud bulwark against the assault of winds, desert, and man. The tenth legion, commanded by the governor of Judea with his eight camps of Roman soldiers and thousands of enslaved prisoners of war, besieged Masada for three years. Jerusalem had already been conquered, and the temple of Solomon had been destroyed for the second time, and yet Masada continued to withstand the attacks. The assault was long and bloody, a war without any hope of victory for the Romans, until Flavius built a huge ramp to get closer to the stronghold. You can still see the ramp today. When the Jews felt the end drawing near, they chose a group of men by lot who had to kill all the others before the Romans entered the stronghold. The last survivor directed the sword against himself and committed suicide. Only the food stocks remained intact as evidence of the fact that the besieged were not starving but were loyal to their oath — they preferred death to slavery. Still today, Israeli army recruits take an oath on the ruins of this fortress, pledging that "Masada will not fall again." By commemorating this terrible and heroic event in their history, the Israelis try to make up for centuries of humiliation and persecution. If you really want to know the new nation of Israel, you should first understand the spirit of Masada. "Shall we always have to fight?" Ben Gurion asked, disheartened, giving voice to one of the most tormenting doubts that plagues Israeli society.

After fighting six wars since 1948, Israel is now waiting for a time of definitive peace with the Arab countries. Since November, 1977, when the historic visit of Egyptian President Anwar Sadat took place in Jerusalem, politicians and diplomats have been exploring every possible way of solving the Middle East problem. The return of the Sinai to the Egyptians on April 25, 1982 occurred peacefully, under the supervision of a multinational force. Despite Israel's attack on Lebanon the following June, the missile bombing by the Iraqis during the Gulf War, and problems of the occupied territories and Palestinian independence, the dialogue has never been interrupted. Everyone hopes that these enemies can, in the near future, shake hands with one other, for no war is eternal. Not only must Masada not fall again but there must be no Masada at all, on either side. In a country where those who believe in miracles are considered to be realistic, it is a duty to believe in peace.

Jerusalem of Gold

The extraordinary union between ancient and modern, between tradition and the future is reflected in the order of the city, where historical monuments stand beside the art of the technological era, giving the urban panorama an extremely diverse and colorful aspect.

The golden city, the eternal city, the city of David: Jerusalem has always been the crossroads between East and West, between different races and worlds. Concentrated in only a few hundred feet are the Wailing Wall, the Omar Mosque, and the Holy Sepulchre — the most important sacred sites of the three principal monotheistic religions. Jerusalem is the natural backdrop for the story of modern civilization and contains a mosaic of culture; this becomes even more evident when one considers the extremely different origins of the population. Jews, Arabs, Muslims, Christians, and Druse all live together, yet maintain intact their own identities.

32 top *Rising near one another on the slopes of the hill of Gethsemane are the Church of Nations, built in 1924, and the Orthodox Church of Saint Mary Magdalene, with its characteristic Russian-style domes.*

32 bottom *In recent years, in the hills surrounding the oldest part of the city, an enormous number of new buildings have been erected, in complete contrast with the simple constructions of the past.*

33 *Located in the oriental quarter is what the Muslims call the "Noble Enclosure," the most sacred place for Muslims and Jews, where the ruins of the walls of the Temple can be found as well as the rock from which Mohammed ascended to heaven.*

The city of faith

34 *Jerusalem has been involved in many a bloody battle, but has always retained its own identity. It is a city with low houses and narrow streets, along which ancient realities live side by side. Also side by side, in the small amount of space available, are the majestic temples of the three main monotheistic religions.*

35 *The eternal city, Jerusalem is considered by many to be the center of the universe. Rising from gently undulating hills furrowed with deep valleys, it is a metropolis geographically divided but at the same time spiritually united; 3,000 years after its founding, Jerusalem possesses, as few other places do, that capability of touching the spirit and inflaming the imagination.*

36-37 *After its reunification in 1967 and subsequent demographic growth, Jerusalem has expanded toward the Judean desert in creating new quarters. Today the city has a population of approximately 400,000 inhabitants.*

The mark of Islam

Built around 699, the Omar Mosque, also known as the Dome of the Rock, is one of the most sacred dwelling places of the Islamic religion and the reason for Mohammed's voyage from Mecca to Jerusalem. The golden dome covers Abraham's rock, on which a footprint indicates the prophet's starting point. The Omar Mosque, an Islamic masterpiece, contains gold and ceramics; majolica panels decorate the upper part of the octagonal buildings and marble, the lower part.

40-41 *Surrounding the Dome of the Rock are other Islamic constructions of different eras — the Chain Cathedral, a miniature version of the Omar Mosque, the Sabeel Qait Bey, a small octagonal structure of the 15th century, and, shown here, the Kadi Burhan ed-Din.*

The other side of Zion

The sacred city of three religions, divided until 1967, Jerusalem is a city whose inhabitants share a common desire for continuity and a reciprocal respect. Jerusalem's population consists of Jews and Muslims, and Christians. Even in the Islamic quarter, which can be reached by means of the Damascus Gate, various components of the Islamic world live together: Palestinians, Egyptian *masri*, Iraqi *ja'abari*, Lebanese, Syrians, and Bedouins, all obeying the precepts of the Mufti, the supreme religious authority.

Jaffa
Jaffa

In Jerusalem, the markets are also a focal point of life. Mahane Yehuda, in the newer part of town, is visited exclusively by Jewish people, whereas the souks, in the Old Town, are frequented by the Arabians. The ancient bazaar near the Jaffa Gate is the most fascinating. The souvenir shops are never ending. Carpets and fabrics are displayed in the doorways, and other articles are heaped inside. The spice shops are even more original. The smell of coffee mixes with the smell of wood and with the characteristic fragrance of falafel, a fried chick-pea pastry.

“The people of The Book”

For the Jewish people, the crucial prayer has remained unaltered through time: “Hear, O Israel, the Lord is our God, the Lord is One.” Judaism is not only theology, belief, or teaching, but above all a way of life that gives concreteness to faith. Today, the most precious guideline for comprehending the country and its mechanisms is the Bible, an ancient book 3,000 years old which has generated an entire race. For the devout, it represents the revelation, both civil and moral, and for laymen it represents Judaism; for both, it contains all one needs to know. That is why, in front of Parliament, there is a shrine that forms an integral part of the National Museum of Israel — “Shrine of The Book” . The famous Dead Sea Scrolls, discovered in 1947 and, without doubt, the most important archeological discovery of Israel’s history, are displayed there. Among these are the complete manuscripts of the book of Isaiah, the study of which has confirmed the historical truth of the Biblical scriptures.

46-47 Surrounding the dome of the Shrine of The Book, are sculptures by Moore, Lipschitz, Rodin and other artists.

48-49 Thousands of Jews are buried in the Mount of Olives cemetery, and, according to the Prophets, the resurrection of the dead will take place here. The small stones on the tombs, placed there by visitors, cannot be removed, according to Jewish law.

חיה לוין

יוסף ווארצעל

So that we do not forget

The Yad Vashem Sanctuary, the temple of memories, silently rises on Remembrance Mount and is dedicated to the millions of Jews brutally slaughtered by the Nazis. On the ninety-nine-foot column in front of the building, the word *Zkor* (remember) is inscribed. Inside is a most impressive and complete documentary collection illustrating the anti-Semitic persecutions from 1933 to 1945. The Ohel Yizkor is a crypt-shrine; under a low cement roof is a stone on which the names of the twenty-one main concentration camps are written. During a brief ceremony, a flame is relit each morning at eleven o'clock. Yad Vashem is a warning to a world which allows catastrophes to repeat themselves.

The Wailing Wall, mirror of the soul

At the foot of the Dome of the Rock and the El-Akjsa Mosque stands the imposing Kotel Maaravi, the Wailing Wall, which originally supported the foundation of Solomon's Temple. No other place in the world is worshipped more by the Jewish people; since the times of the Roman occupation, followed by the Diaspora of the Jews, the people of Israel come here to pray and to demonstrate their sorrow over the destruction of the House of God. In 1967, when Jerusalem was reunited, the old structures concealing part of the Wailing Wall were torn down, leaving a large open space to accommodate all the people who visit each day. This sacred place is an open-air synagogue, and men have to cover their heads. Since the orthodox Jewish religion does not allow men and women to pray together, the wall has been divided into two parts.

54-55 *A young boy is absorbed in reading the Torah during his Bar Mitzvah ceremony in front of the Wailing Wall. For Jewish children, this is the equivalent to Holy Confirmation and represents the passage into adult life.*

Life in observance of tradition

Although united by a common faith in the *Torah* (the first five books of the Bible), the Jewish people differ as far as customs and practices are concerned; there are reform, conservative, and orthodox Jews. Today, as in the past, those belonging to the orthodox community of Jerusalem scrupulously observe the Talmudic law, (a collection of comments and laws handed down from generation to generation since the 5th century), living only in prayer and study, refusing the temptations of the modern world, of wealth and of any ostentation whatsoever. Some of them even refuse to accept the new State of Israel, declaring that because of its foundation, the coming of the Messiah is not foreseen, and consequently, in the temple they actually weep for the fall of Zion. The men still wear long, black coats and wide-brimmed hats beneath which long "earlocks" appear. The women dress in a simple fashion. The children are allowed to play very few games; their duty is to study the Holy Scriptures in the Talmudic schools in order to perpetuate their orthodox faith. Among these schools, the Talmud Torah Shomrei Hachomot School is one of the most severe in the preparation of youngsters for a life dedicated to religion and to study.

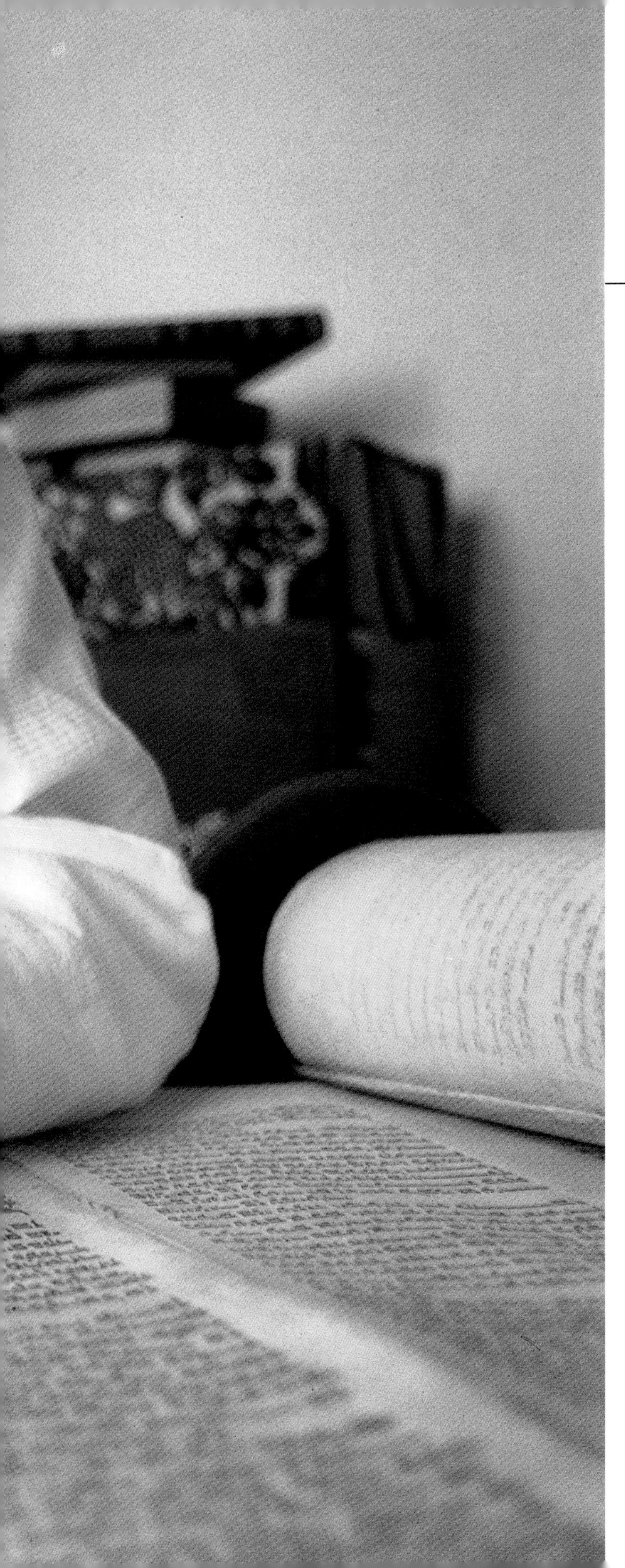

Mea She'Arim, an alcove in a world apart

58-59 *Many orthodox communities live together in Mea She'arim. Posters indicate that decent clothing should be worn by all and that Shabbat must be respected. The inhabitants of Mea She'arim strictly follow the Holy Commandments. Continuity of tradition is guaranteed by studying the Holy Scriptures, and in the Talmudic schools, the scribes continuously recopy the Scriptures.*

The places of the spirit

60 top left *A black dome covers the Holy Sepulchre.*

60 bottom left *The Via Dolorosa starts at the Gate of the Convent of the Scourging.*

60 top right *A Catholic procession takes place on Good Friday along the Road of Sorrows.*

60 bottom right *A Greek Orthodox procession is held near the Holy Sepulchre, in celebration of Palm Sunday.*

61 *An Easter Friday procession along the roads of the Old Town.*

In Jerusalem, the various religions appear to be complementary rather than adversarial, blending in a unique mixture of liturgies and vestments. It is no wonder that numerous creeds share joint ownership of most of the Christian holy dwelling places. Although at one time, this type of fraternal existence was not possible, today an ecumenical spirit seems to prevail. The Christian institutes, many and prosperous, are generally occupied in teaching and are open to all.

The basilica of the Holy Sepulchre is situated where the very center of the Christian faith has been located for centuries, and today remains an important site for pilgrimages. There, where the Golgotha was located, Emperor Constantine had a magnificent basilica built as well as a place for Jesus's sepulchre. It was the most beautiful and richest church of all Jerusalem, but it was destroyed in 614 by Persian invaders. It was rebuilt and modified several times, but its structure dates back mainly to the Crusades. Inside, in addition to Christ's tomb, a chapel was built in the spot where Our Lady witnessed Christ's resurrection. Its architecture is heterogeneous. The Franciscan monks take care of the church — with numerous disputes, however, with the Greek Orthodox, the Armenians, and the Copts. Each Christian community looks after its own chapels and altars, celebrating different religious functions at different times of the day. Furthermore, each maintains its own sector. At first sight, the Holy Sepulchre basilica appears somewhat gloomy, but in spite of the first impression, the church glows in all its incomparable splendor.

64, 65 bottom *Saint James's Cathedral, in the heart of the Old Town, was consecrated according to the Armenian liturgy. Converted to the Christian faith in 303 and present in the Holy Land as guardians of the Holy Sepulchre, together with Catholics and the Orthodox, the Armenians venerate the saint who lead the first Judean-Christian community of Israel. The traditional pointed hat worn by Armenian prelates represents Mount Ararat.*

65 top *The Russian Orthodox creed is present in Jerusalem through the Church of Saint Mary Magdalene, built between 1885 and 1888 by Czar Alexander III, in memory of his wife Maria Alexandrovina. The Russian Christian congregation, among the most secluded, is among those involved in contention for the holy dwelling places.*

66-67 The silence during breakfast in the refectory of the Church of Saint Mary Magdalene is interrupted only by the reading of the Gospel. The church and the surrounding fields are cared for by Russian Orthodox nuns.

68-69 Jerusalem is the Holy City for Jews, Christians, and Muslims — land of pilgrimages and contrasts. Although they live together in apparent chaos, the desire for continuity exists, making Jerusalem not only a city for mankind but also for reflection.

The roots of the world

The country is not large; hence, there are no great distances between cities. In practice, any historical, archeological, or tourist spot can be reached from Tel Aviv or Jerusalem within a day. Its size notwithstanding, Israel's territory is surprisingly varied.

The traces of its more than thousand-year-old history are visible everywhere, whereas its landscape is subordinate to the climate and to physical characteristics different from those of any other country in the world.

Even as far as climate is concerned, Israel reflects its complicated geographical and ethnic situation, alternating from a barren zone to a temperate zone within a few miles. Along the coast there is a dry, hot climate from April to the end of November, and during the hottest months of July and August, there are often cool sea breezes. Across the country, winter is very brief — November to February; the temperature is mild, the rain is frequent, and snow is rare. Further south, the heat is intense from May to late September, so that in the Negev desert and the Dead Sea basin, the temperature often exceeds 40° C.

70 top *A splendid Corinthian capital of the Augustan era recalls the ancient splendor of Caesarea, the most monumental archeological site in of all Israel.*

70 bottom *The Druse village of Majdal Shams, in the Meli Valley, stretches out towards Mount Hermon, 9,234 feet high and divided between Israel, Syria, and Lebanon.*

71 *The landscape near Timna, where King Solomon's copper mines were once situated, is among the most magical in Israel; the formation known as Mushroom Rock is pictured here.*

Golan, the fertile frontier

72 Bordered on the west by Lake Tiberias and the Jordan, on the north by Mount Hermon, and on the south and east by the Yarmouk and Raqqad rivers, the Golan Heights forms the extreme northern border of the State of Israel. In this territory, famous for its fertile land, more than 11,000 people live in approximately twenty new villages erected since 1967. The Golan Heights is entirely dominated by the imposing silhouette of Mount Hermon, a skier's paradise, with snow falling rarely between November to March.

73 top *One of the main features of the Golan Heights is an abundance of springs of water, even though they are located in the Syrian desert. This explains the existence of a few small lakes, such as Masada Lake.*

73 bottom *A popular Arab saying describes Mount Hermon: "At its feet, eternal summer; at its sides, spring; at its shoulders, autumn; at its head, winter." In fact, it is the only area in Israel with an alpine climate, and it undergoes the greatest changes of temperature between summer and winter.*

The springs of the Jordan

74-75 The slopes of Mount Hermon are full of small springs, which come together to form the Jordan. Throughout the entire area, the continuous sound of waterfalls and streams can be heard; the Banjas Springs are one of the most fascinating natural attractions of the country, well known for thousands of years and written about by the Romans and in the Gospel.

The Jordan Valley, the Biblical Eden

The extremely fertile Jordan Valley enjoys a very mild climate even in winter. The flora is varied and includes bananas, mangos, and avocados. Israeli agriculture, particularly in the kibbutz, has very much improved in recent years; fruit orchards, vegetable gardens, and greenhouses, irrigated by the Jordan, furnish high quality products in considerable amounts to both local and foreign markets.

Lake Tiberias, the jewel of Galilee

Lake Tiberias, more than sixty-six feet below sea level in the heart of Galilee, is situated between hills covered with abundant, sub-tropical vegetation. The Jordan, rising from Mount Hermon and flowing into the Sea of Galilee, gives life to the lake.

On its banks, Jesus preached to the Apostles. Nearby, the miracle of the loaves and fishes is said to have taken place, and a little farther away, at Capernaum, Saint Peter lived.

78 *A modern Franciscan basilica, built by Italian monks, adorns the top of Mount Tabor, which dominates Jezreel Valley, where the disciples saw Jesus's face lit by a supernatural light.*

79 *The Sea of Galilee has always been extremely fascinating to mankind; 2,000 years ago, Josephus described the scene surrounding the lake as "incommensurable for its natural beauty."*

Memories of ancient vicissitudes

80 top *Clinging to the highest hill of the region, the colossal fortress of Belvoir overlooks the entire Jordan Valley.*

80 bottom *The ruins of numerous castles such as the Subeibe in Galilee remain as reminders of one of the most bloody periods in the history of the Jewish race.*

81 top *The city of Capernaum, in Upper Galilee, boasts one of the most beautiful synagogues in the country; dating back to the fourth century B.C., it is evidence of the influence of Hellenistic and Jewish art.*

81 bottom *The spectacular Roman theater of Beth She'an in the Jordan Valley could hold 8,000 spectators; even today, this marvelous structure is known for its excellent acoustics.*

82-83 *The Wadi Kelt is a deep valley into which the mountains of the Judean desert seem to flow and which cradles the Greek Orthodox monastery of Saint George.*

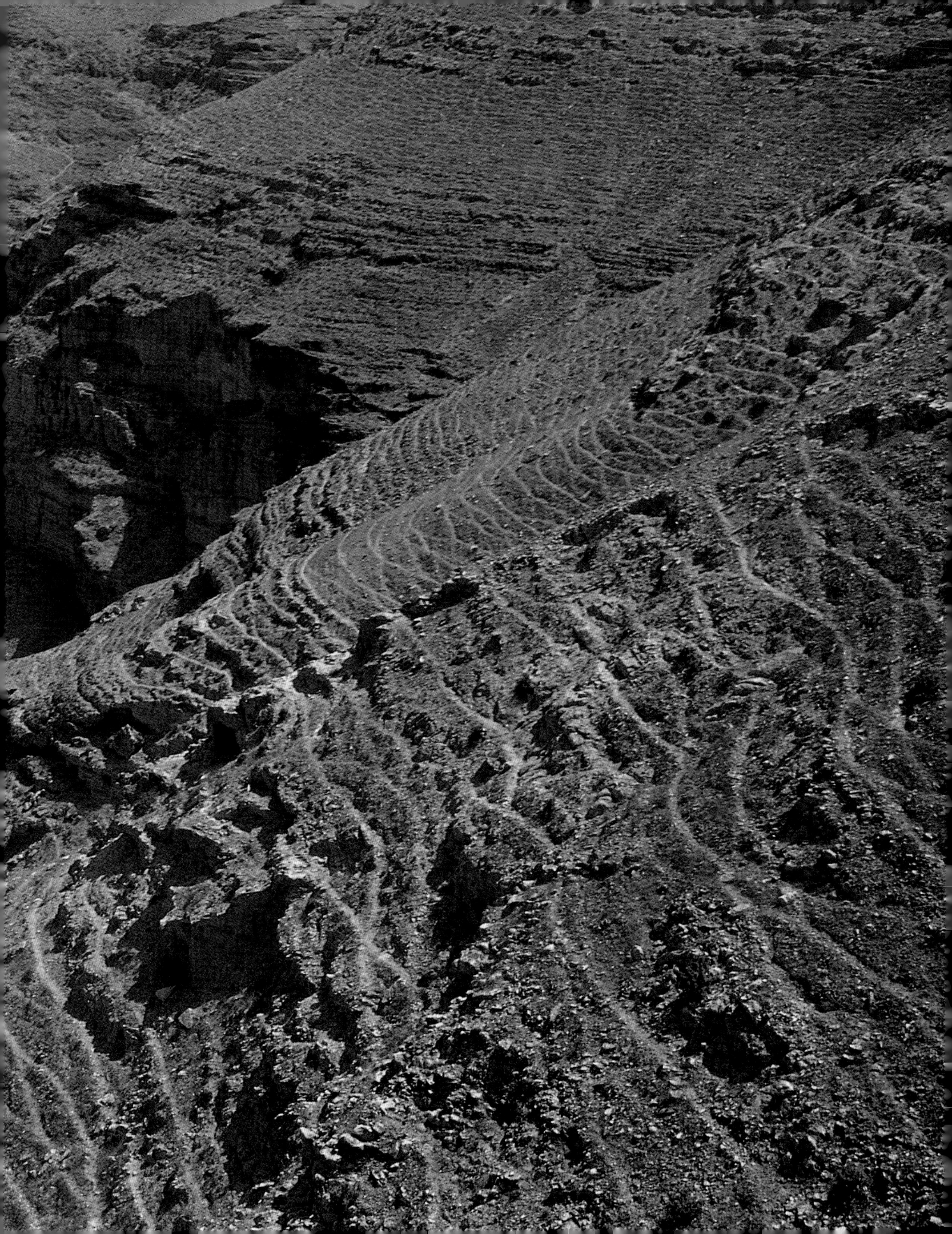

The Dead Sea, a spectacular oddity of nature

The Dead Sea, fifty miles long and no more than ten miles wide, is located in the deepest tectonic cavity of the world, at approximately 1,296 feet below sea level.

84 top *The very arid rocky desert surrounding the Dead Sea is interrupted only by the green of the kibbutz and the thermal resorts; the beneficial effects of mud-baths and mineral waters to the skin have been well known since ancient times. Legend states that Cleopatra very much appreciated these effects.*

84 bottom *The En Gedi oasis, with its springs and luxuriant vegetation, is a heavenly kingdom in the middle of the barren Dead Sea.*

84 right *In the mountains behind the Qumran ruins near the Dead Sea, there are several caves, where, in 1947, two Bedouin shepherds found seven jars containing Biblical manuscripts, the most ancient found to date. The Dead Sea Scrolls are displayed in the Jerusalem Museum.*

85 *En Bokek is one of the most popular tourist sites of the Dead Sea, with modern swimming and thermal resorts.*

מים עמוקים
DEEP WATER

The Dead Sea, an anomaly

Deep within a cavity of the Earth since the African continent detached itself from Turkey and the Middle East, ten times saltier than any other sea, so dense that it's practically impossible to sink into, with no humid winds ever reaching it, the Dead Sea is in fact only a lake, a lake of pale blue water from the Jordan without any form of life whatsoever. In the water are high concentrations of bromide, magnesium, calcium, sodium, and potassium, and if one swims in this water, in order to avoid irritation to the skin, a shower is necessary immediately afterwards. However, because of these minerals, the water of the Dead Sea is rich in therapeutic properties and is utilized by various thermal resorts in curing skin diseases and respiratory problems.

Masada, pride of a nation

The Masada Fortress rises up from a rock on the western shore of the Dead Sea. The main buildings and the fortifications of the fortress,1,968 feet long and 300 to 550 wide, were built in 37 B.C. by King Herod. The entire plateau was surrounded by a wall reinforced with thirty-seven towers. Inside were a palace, an arsenal, lodgings for 1,000 soldiers, and an ample water supply, thanks to huge underground tanks filled with rain water or by means of an aqueduct. The vast area of the plateau was cultivated, and the food stuffs were preserved in large covered warehouses. After Herod, the fortress was besieged by Roman soldiers, and later, at the beginning of the Jewish-Roman war, by the zealots. In 73 B.C., Flavius Silva's army beseiged it. Four years later, Roman soldiers opened a breach in a wall of the fortress, and the besieged, approximately 1,000 in number, preferred to commit suicide rather than surrender.

88 top *Discovered among the ruins of the Masada Fortress were the ruins of the columbarium, a funerary building, the walls of which are entirely filled with niches into which funeral urns were placed.*

88 center *The zealots had to improvise as best they could, given that they did not have the necessary equipment. For example, they built a simple oven against a splendid mosaic wall in the royal palace.*

88 bottom *The thermal system of Masada demonstrates an evident Roman influence: the calidarium, a room for taking hot baths, still preserves the pavement support, a typical system for heating a room.*

89 *Through patient restoration and research, it has been possible to save many extremely important buildings and exhibits, including walls, fortifications, mosaics, columns, and wall paintings. Many common objects have also been found, including large round stones used as bullets against the enemy.*

90-91 *Masada is not only a very interesting archeological site, but also an important symbol of the Israeli national culture. For this reason, when commencing their military service at the swearing-in ceremony held at the fortress, recruits swear that "Masada will never fall again."*

The Negev desert, a continuous challenge

92-93 *In only a few years, the obstinate yet determined farmers of the kibbutz revolutionized the landscape of large areas of the Negev desert, bringing in water where it did not exist and thus permitting the existence of modern agriculture.*

94-95 *The Dead Sea is one of the most barren areas on our planet; the level of humidity reaches a maximum of fifteen per cent, and there are less than two inches of rainfall annually.*

96 top *In the heart of the Negev desert rises the ancient city of Avdat, where, across the centuries, majestic Roman palaces were built, along with two large Byzantine churches and a fortress. The archeological excavations that led to the discovery of the ruins of Avdat began in 1950.*

96 bottom *En Avdat is one of the natural wonders of the Negev. Hidden at the bottom of a steep gorge is a natural pool; its water, rising from an underground source, is contained in a frame of rare beauty.*

97 top *In the Negev desert, there are three natural craters, their origin still unknown. According to certain theories, they are the result of ancient volcanic activities. According to others, they are chasms produced by the clashing of enormous meteorites. Machtesh Ramon, the largest of the three, is twenty-five miles long and seven miles wide.*

97 bottom *Near Eilat, in the Negev region, there are two enormous rocks known as King Solomon's Pillars. They are the result of a violent tectonic movement, which occurred in prehistoric times when the earth moved upward.*

The weaving of a single mosaic

Israel is still a young nation, but in the course of its brief history, its population has grown significantly. From 1948 to 1952, the Israeli population more than doubled, growing from 650,000 to 1,400,000 people. Today, the inhabitants number approximately 4,500,000, and five of every six are Jewish. Israel's society is mainly industrialized, with more than eighty-four per cent of the population located in the major urban centers; nearly twenty-five per cent of the population is situated in Tel Aviv. The rural community has gradually decreased since 1954, as people tend to abandon the countryside for the cities.

98 top *Wrapped in an atmosphere of ancestral abandonment and oriental fascination, Akko seems out of place in the frantic landscape of a young nation, as a city where one can enjoy life without haste.*

98 bottom *Built on the hills of Judea, Hebron is probably one of the most ancient cities in the world. It is seat of Aaram el Khalil sanctuary, that retains the tombs of Abraham and Sarah, Isaac and Rebecca, Jacob and Leah.*

99 *The modern urbanization and the chaotic aspect of Tel Aviv signify its recent origin, dating to the beginning of the century. In complete contrast with Jerusalem, the capital of eternity, Tel Aviv appears to be the capital of activity, the center for all political, social, and administrative activities, the cultural and economic center. In other words, Tel Aviv is Israel's engine.*

Tel Aviv, Israel's metropolis

100 *The "White Square" (top) and the new Synagogue (bottom) are among the most recent architectural achievements in Tel Aviv.*

101 *The marina across from the Kikar Atarim commercial complex is the largest in the Middle East.*

102-103 *Founded in 1909, Tel Aviv, with 500,000 inhabitants, is the most populous city in Israel.*

104 *Modern Tel Aviv is the liveliest city in Israel; in only a few decades, the original heart of the city has grown to become an urban center, dynamic and throbbing, with spacious streets filled with traffic, shops, cinemas, boutiques, bars, cultural centers, art galleries, and museums. Tel Aviv is full of life and moves to the nervous, hectic beat typical of a large metropolis. The restaurants and bars are open-air cafés visited day and night by artists, writers, and journalists.*

105 top *The entire coastline of Tel Aviv is dominated by an impressive number of modern buildings and luxury hotels.*

105 center *Tel Aviv's beaches, well equipped and always clean, are continuously maintained and hence are an ideal site for residents and visitors.*

105 bottom *The modern Mann Auditorium, near the theater, is the home of Israel's Philharmonic Orchestra.*

Haifa, the tolerant

106 *Overlooking Haifa's panorama, the golden dome of Bahai Temple shines in the center of a luxuriant Persian garden.*

107 top *Haifa is situated on 7,500 hectares of land and is populated by 250,000 inhabitants.*

107 bottom *Haifa has progressively covered the layers of Mount Carmel, whose splendor was extolled by the Prophet Isaiah.*

Situated between the sea and Mount Carmel, not only is Haifa the most important commercial and tourist port of Israel, but also an active industrial center. The Technion Institute (for scientific and technological research) is located here. The urban area stretches from the commercial quarters of the port to the elegant residential quarters and gardens near Mount Carmel, from the bay up to the surrounding hills. Haifa is a lively, rich city; all the commerce from the Gezrael Valley is concentrated in this port.

Tiberias, the city on the lake

A Roman city famous for its thermal water, winter resorts, and tourist centers, Tiberias is famous beyond Israel's borders. It was founded by Herod Antipas, son of Herod the Great, who named it after Emperor Tiberius. When the Romans expelled the Jews from Jerusalem, Tiberias became the Hebrew center. Because of its geographical position, the city has a stormy past; it was dominated by Byzantines, Crusaders, Saracens, and Turks — each leaving their traces. Among the most important monuments are the tombs of Rabbi Meir Baal Maness and Rabbi Akiba; these are sacred Hebrew shrines for pilgrimages.

Caesarea, a reminder of imperial magnificence

The name Caesarea evokes the joys that this city, forgotten for many centuries, knew when Herod the Great dedicated it to Caesar and adorned it with the precious marble monuments whose ruins are still present today. During its history, Ceasarea had always been involved in bloody wars because of its strategic position. The Crusaders arrived in 1101 and built an enormous defense apparatus, which, unfortunately, has been reduced to a rubble. Various excavations, which began thirty years ago, have revealed important Roman traces, including an amphitheater, a theater, city walls, and a medieval stronghold.

112 left *Shown here is the long portico leading to the Crusaders' stronghold.*

112 right *Among the most interesting monuments of Caesarea are the Roman theater and the fortress built by Saint Louis' Crusaders.*

113 *Elegant pointed arches support the ceiling of a huge hall in the Crusaders' stronghold.*

Acre, a city with a checkered past

The ancient port of Acre, in the northern part of Acre Gulf, was conquered many times. It belonged to the Egyptians, the Assyrians, the Persians, and the Romans, was conquered by the Arabs in 638, and in 1191 by Richard the Lion-Heart, whereupon it became the center of the Crusades. Later, it was controlled by the Knights of Saint John and was their capital, until, in 1291, it was reconquered by the Muslims, who let it become completely run down. Only in the 18th century was Acre revived by the Turks, and in 1799, with the help of the British fleet, it withstood a siege by Napoleon. An Arab city, Acre was conquered in 1948 by the Israeli army. Today there are approximately 40,000 inhabitants, two thirds of whom are Jewish.

114 *After Israel's Declaration of Independence, the city quickly retrieved its function as a port, developing an intensive industrial activity. In spite of this, it has maintained its fascination as an ancient medieval center because of its numerous monuments.*

115 *The Ottoman architectural style is a characteristic of Acre, thanks to the construction work carried out by Pasha Ahmend el-Jazzar in the 18th century. The splendid mosque named after the Pasha was built in 1781, and is the largest in Israel and a spiritual center of extreme importance for the Muslim community.*

Silent, and surrounded by walls erected by the Crusaders, Acre appears to be meditating on the vastness of the Mediterranean Sea. The ancient stones, part of the centuries-old history, the Knights Palace, the underground crypt, the Pasha Jazzar Mosque — all tell the story of battles, sieges, and destruction. Among the most important activities carried on here today are the extraction of an important natural coloring — a purple dye — and the glass industry. The Roman historian, Pliny, credited the city, then named Colonia Claudia Felix, with the discovery of the technique for the manufacture of glass. Mentioned many times in the Bible and by the Egyptians, Acre maintains intact the mystery of the Arabian Far East, visible mainly in the narrow streets of the souk or at the quays of the medieval port, where the fishermen unload the fruits of their labor each day.

116 top *In the countryside surrounding Acre, one can see the slender arches of an aqueduct built by the Turks as a water supply for the city.*

116 center *These enclosures were part of a particular type of hotel built in the Far East for caravans. One of these, the Khan El Umdan, in the heart of the Old Town, had a covered double tunnel and a high tower.*

116 bottom *Supported by tall pointed arches, the crypt of the Crusaders' stronghold represents one of the most interesting examples of medieval Gothic architecture in the Holy Land.*

117 *In the ancient part of Acre, dominated by the minarets of two mosques, one has the impression of being in an Arabian city where life passes according to ancient rhythms.*

Nazareth, city of the Annunciation

In Arabiac and Hebrew, the name Nazareth means "guardian," and the name perhaps originally referred to the strategic location of the village, situated on the top of a hill dominating the Esdrelon Valley. Today, however, it appears to follow the charge that history has given it; it has become the guardian of the Christian tradition. According to the Holy Scriptures, Mary announced the birth of Jesus in this village, and for this reason, the first Christians built their church here. It was replaced by a Byzantine basilica and then by a Crusader basilica, and now only ruins remain. In 1730, the Franciscan monks began to build a new church, which was destroyed in 1955 in order to make space for the grand complex designed by the Italian architect, Giovanni Muzio.

118 left *Completed on the eve of the Six Day War, the Annunciation Basilica is the largest Christian church in the Middle East and was financed by the State of Israel. The modern building was built near the cave were the archangel Gabriel visited the Virgin Mary.*

118 right *The Annunciation Basilica, built over twenty years, has incorporated features of previous Byzantine churches.*

119 *Only recently has Nazareth developed a significant urban section. The city has a rather complicated ethnic and religious aspect. Apart from the Muslims, who live in the Old Town, and the Jews, who live in the new quarter, there are also numerous Christian, Arabian, Catholic, and Greek Orthodox communities, each with its own place of worship.*

Bethlehem, cradle of Christianity

Bethlehem is situated six miles from Jerusalem in the midst of a fertile area filled with olive trees, grapevines, and wheat — hence its original name Ephrata (fertility). According to ancient Jewish history, David's family came from Bethlehem, which is always mentioned as a small, poor village. Tradition states that Jesus was born in Bethlehem, and Saint Jerome described a cave which quickly became one of the main holy dwelling places of the Christian faith. On the site where the Redeemer was born, Saint Helen, Emperor Constantine's mother, had a large church built in 330 — probably the oldest in the world.

120 top left *As occurred many times in the Holy Land, the Christian holy dwelling places were built on the sites of earlier holy places; the church of Saint Catherine, although modern, was originally a medieval cloister.*

120 top right *Bethlehem is not holy solely for Christians; the Jewish religion celebrates here the memory of Rachel — Jacob's wife.*

120 bottom *Connected to the Nativity Cave, the Church of Saint Catherine was built in 1882; each year, Christmas Mass is celebrated here and is broadcast worldwide.*

121 *Diverse religious symbols adorn the architecture of the Bethlehem landscape.*

122 top *In the Cave of the Nativity, a silver star in the pavement marks the site of the blessed event. On it is simply inscribed:* Hic de Vergine Maria Jesus nata est. *Here, from the Virgin Mary, Jesus was born.*

122 bottom *Over many centuries of pilgrimages, the various Christian creeds have left their own testimonies in the Church of the Nativity in an explosion of votive lamps.*

123 *The Cave of the Nativity, which belongs to the Greek Orthodox monks, is small, and the walls are partially covered by marble. Situated in a small apse is the altar of the Birth of Christ, adorned with fifteen silver lamps, each belonging to a different Christian creed, and a silver star. On either side is a smaller altar — one representing the manger where Jesus was born, and the other, the three kings.*

Eilat, the submerged paradise

The city of Eilat is situated in the most southern part of Israel on the Akaba Gulf. In recent years this city has become a flourishing tourist center, visited mainly by deep-sea divers, who come to explore the spectacular coral beds comparable only to those of the tropics. Eilat is famous for its submarine observatory, which includes an aquarium, a museum, and a "tower," from inside which visitors can view the sea world directly.

LUCKY DIVERS

L'AMIE

Photo Credits:

Marcello Bertinetti/Archivio White Star:
Cover, backcover, pages 1, 2-3, 4-5, 6, 7, 10-11, 19 top, 26, 27, 28 bottom, 32 top, 32 bottom, 34, 35, 36-37, 38, 39, 40-41, 42, 43,44,45,46,47, 48-49, 50, 51, 52, 53, 54-55, 56, 57, 58, 59, 60, 61, 62 top, 62 bottom, 63, 65, 66-67, 80 top, 90-91, 92 top, 94-95, 101, 105 bottom, 112, 128.

Cesare Gerolimetto/Archivio White Star:
Pages 8-9, 12-13, 18 left, 22, 23 bottom, 28 top, 29 top, 29 bottom, 30-31, 62 center, 68-69, 70, 71 72, 73 top, 74, 75, 76, 77, 78, 79, 81 top, 82-83, 84 bottom, 85, 86, 92 bottom, 93, 97, 99, 100, 102-103, 104, 105 top and center, 106-107, 108-109, 110, 111, 118 left, 123, 124, 125.

G.B.A. Communication/SIE:
Page 88 center and bottom.

Richard T. Nowitz/Apa Photo Agency:
Pages 24-25, 64, 87.

Jean-Charles Pinheira:
Pages 16, 17, 18 right, 19 center and bottom, 20-21, 23 top, 80 bottom, 88 top, 96, 98, 112 right, 113, 114, 116, 118 right, 119, 120, 121, 122, 126-127.

M. Zur/ZEFA: Page 117.

ZEFA: Pages 4-15, 73 bottom, 115.

Printed in Singapore
Color separations by Magenta, Lit. Con., Singapore.